KALEIDOSCOPE

COMETS, ASTEROIDS, AND METEORITES

by

Roy A. Gallant

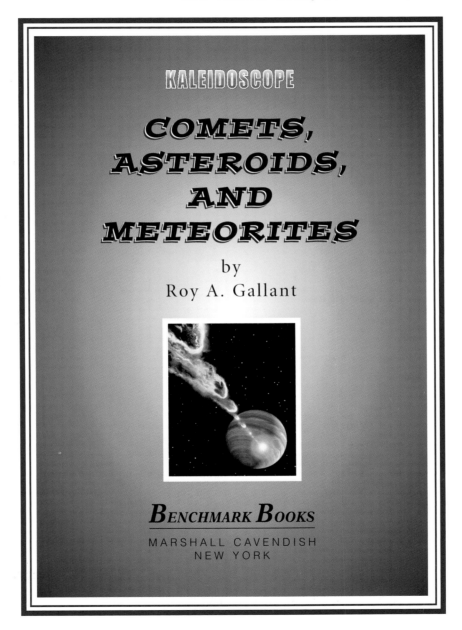

BENCHMARK BOOKS

MARSHALL CAVENDISH
NEW YORK

Series consultant:
Dr. Jerry LaSala, Chairman
Department of Physics
University of Southern Maine

Benchmark Books
Marshall Cavendish Corporation
99 White Plains Road
Tarrytown, New York 10591-9001

Library of Congress Cataloging-in-Publication Data
Comets, asteroids, and meteorites / by Roy A. Gallant.
     p. cm. — (Kaleidoscope)
Includes bibliographical references and index.
Summary: An introduction to the celestial phenomena of asteroids, meteoroids and meteorites, and comets.
ISBN 0-7614-1034-1
1. Comets—Juvenile literature. 2. Asteroids—Juvenile literature. 3. Meteorites—Juvenile literature. [1. Comets. 2. Asteroids.
3. Meteorites.] I. Title. II. Kaleidoscope (Tarrytown, N.Y.)
QB721.5 .G35 2001   523.5—dc21   99-047492

Photo research by Candlepants Incorporated
Cover photo: Photo Researchers/Julian Baum/Science Photo Library
The photographs in this book are used by permission and through the courtesy of:Photo research by Candlepants Inc.
Photo Researchers, Inc.: /Sauzereau O/Explorer, 5; Roger Harris/Science Photo Library, 9; Lynette Cook/SPL, 10; Julian
Baum/SPL, 13, 33, 38, 41; NASA/SPL, 14; /George Gerster, 17; Detlev Van Ravenswaay/SPL, 18; /Frank Zullo, 21; Joe
Tucciarone/SPL, 25. Dr. Seth Shostak/SPL, 29; /Kent Wood, 30, 37; David Hardy/SPL, 34; Novosti Press Agency/SPL, 42.
CORBIS: Bettmann, 6; Jonathan Blair, 26.

Printed in Italy

6 5 4 3 2 1

CONTENTS

SPACE JUNK

The Solar System is filled with tons of space junk. In addition to the Sun, the nine planets, and more than sixty moons, there are millions upon millions of asteroids and comets. The *asteroids* are chunks of rock and metal that tumble through space in orbits mostly between Mars and Jupiter. *Comets*, on the other hand, lie near the outer edges of the Solar System. Described as "dirty snowballs" by one astronomer, comets are ice loosely packed together. The asteroids and comets are made up of material left over after the planets formed some 4.6 billion years ago.

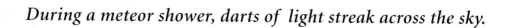

During a meteor shower, darts of light streak across the sky.

Astronomers in the 1700s. The man on the left is measuring the height of the Sun above the horizon with an instrument called a quadrant. The one on the right is using a long-tube refracting telescope.

THE CASE OF THE MISSING PLANET

In 1772, the German astronomer Johann Bode thought that something was wrong with the Solar System. A planet seemed to be missing. Some simple math showed him how the planets were regularly spaced —with one exception. There should have been a planet in the wide gap between Mars and Jupiter, but there wasn't one. Why not?

To solve the mystery, in the late 1700s a group of German astronomers turned their telescopes toward the sky and searched every inch of space between Mars and Jupiter. They called themselves the Celestial Police. But it was a Sicilian astronomer named Giuseppi Piazzi who turned out to be the better detective. On January 1, 1801, he discovered something in the "gap," almost exactly where Bode believed the missing planet should be. It turned out to be a midget planet only 568 miles (914 kilometers) wide, about one-quarter the size of the Moon.

Giuseppi Piazzi had made a very important discovery. Johann Bode's missing planet turned out to be an asteroid.

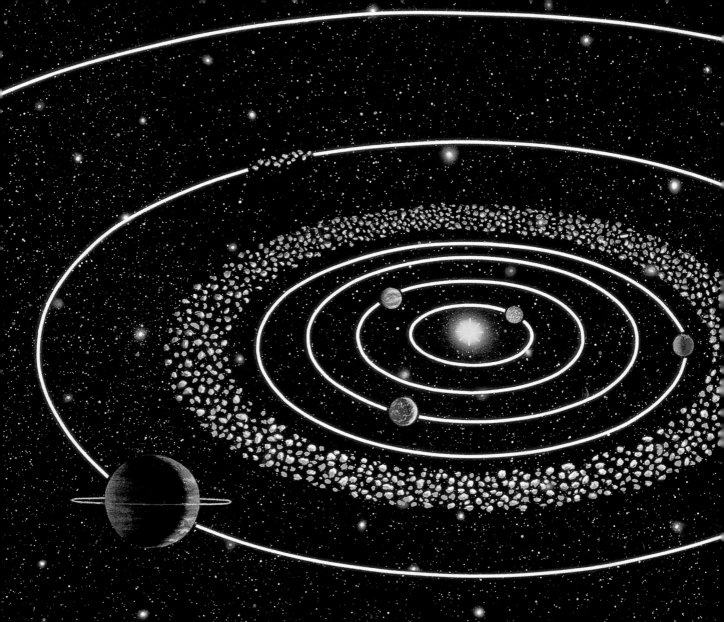

Thousands of asteroids orbit the Sun mainly between Mars and Jupiter. From time to time, they smash into each other and break apart. Often the pieces fly out of their orbit and crash into Earth.

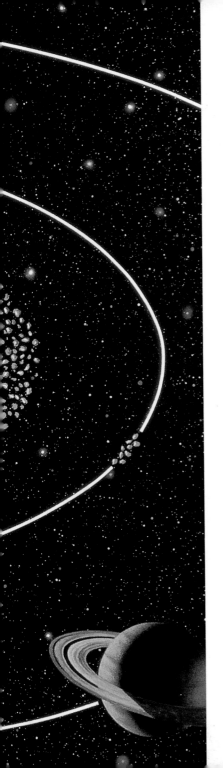

Astronomers began to ask when and how this mere pebble of a planet came to be. Piazzi's midget was given the name Ceres, and it became the first asteroid ever discovered. A year later, Heinrich Olbers found a second asteroid in the gap. It was named Pallas and was half the size of Ceres. Then in 1804, Juno was sighted. It was only half the size of Pallas. In 1807, Vesta—with a diameter of 311 miles (500 kilometers)—was added to the list. Vesta is the brightest asteroid and can be seen without a telescope. These were just the first of many discoveries. By 1890, astronomers had found more than three hundred asteroids.

Considering their work done, the Celestial Police turned in their badges and moved on to other cases. Since then, we have spotted more than 20,000 asteroids and have mapped the orbits of more than 6,000. A typical asteroid orbits the Sun in about five Earth years at a distance of 200 to 300 million miles (320 to 480 million kilometers) from the Sun.

The peanut asteroid, or perhaps two separate asteroids spinning around each other. Named Hector, this pair travels along Jupiter's orbit, well outside the Asteroid Belt.

13

Full of craters, asteroid Ida was photographed by the Galileo *space probe on its way to Jupiter in 1993. Ida is 32 miles (52 kilometers) long.*

But where do asteroids come from? Astronomers now think that the strong pull of Jupiter's gravity prevented a large planet from forming nearby. Instead, many smaller planet pieces formed. For millions of years these chunks of rock and metal have been smashing into each other like bumper cars. The larger asteroids, such as Ida and Gaspra, have many craters. Some are covered with nicks and pock marks. Others grind themselves down from the size of mountains to boulders and finally to tiny pebbles.

15

THE NIGHT THE SKY FELL DOWN

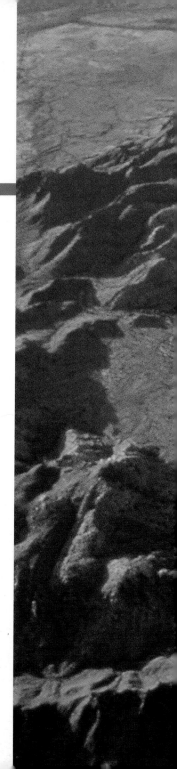

On the night of November 13, 1833, people fled their houses in terror. The sky was lit up with thousands of shooting stars, or *meteors*. "The stars fell like flakes of snow," one witness said. Another feared that when the meteor storm ended there wouldn't be any stars left in the sky. When asteroids collide, pieces are chipped off and sent flying off in new orbits. When they are soaring through space, we call these fragments *meteoroids*. They can be as small as a speck of dust or larger than a train car.

Sometimes, meteors crash into Earth. Then they are called meteorites.
This crater in Australia was made thousands of years ago.

A slice of the Imilac meteorite, found in Chile in 1822. A mixture of metal and rock, meteorites survive the swift and hot journey through Earth's air and land on the planet's surface.

Every day more than a thousand meteoroids rain down through Earth's air at speeds from about 12 to 25 miles (20 to 40 kilometers) per second. As they do, they are heated until they burn up. We see them only for a moment as a streak of light we call a meteor. If one survives its journey down through the air and strikes the ground, we call it a *meteorite*. There is a meteor shower nearly every month of the year. During a good "storm," you can count as many as fifty meteors an hour. During the storm of 1833, people saw up to 10,000 meteors an hour.

There are three kinds of meteorites—iron, stony, and stony-irons. The irons are a blend of iron and nickel. The stony ones are mostly silicate rock with a little iron and nickel mixed in. Some stony meteorites contain the heavy rock basalt. The stony-irons are about half rock and half metal.

THE HAIRY STARS

While asteroids and meteoroids are the same—except for size—comets are in a class by themselves. Long ago comets were called "hairy stars" because of their long tails. Once people were just as terrified by comets as they were by meteors. They believed comets caused earthquakes, famine, and wars. In 1910, when the most famous comet of all, Halley's Comet, made a return visit, people thought they would be poisoned by the comet's gas tail. Dishonest merchants made lots of money selling comet pills they claimed would offer protection. Today we know comets are harmless, unless one is heading straight for us!

Halley's Comet sweeps around the Sun and passes Earth once every seventy-six years. This photograph was taken of the comet's last flyby (lower left) in 1986.

PARTS OF A COMET

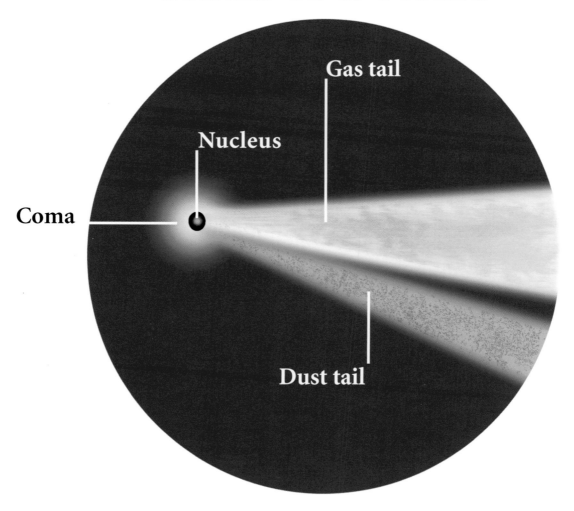

A comet is a spongy ball of ice mixed up with a lot of carbon. The ball is called the comet's *nucleus*. The nucleus of Halley's Comet is shaped like a giant peanut about 9 miles long by 5 miles wide (15 by 8 kilometers). When a comet sweeps in from outer space and loops around the Sun, its icy nucleus starts to heat up. This causes the outer layers of ice to change into a cocoon of gases that surround the nucleus. Called the *coma*, it may be some 120,000 miles (193,000 kilometers) across.

A comet's double tail streams off behind its nucleus and coma.

As the comet nears the Sun, it sends off strong jets of gas and dust, mostly from the coma. The matter boils off and trails behind the comet as a double tail millions of miles long. The movement of light rays out into space always keeps the tail pointing away from the Sun. One part of the tail is made of dust grains and shines with a yellow light. The other part is made of charged atoms called *ions*. The ion part of the tail comes from the coma and shines with a pale blue glow. The gases of a comet's tail are so thin that one astronomer said they are "as close to nothing as something can get."

Gases from a comet's coma are pushed out into a long double tail.

This photograph, taken in 1910, shows some of the damage at Tunguska.

NEAR-EARTH OBJECTS

At 7:15 on the morning of June 30, 1908, a large object from space entered Earth's atmosphere and exploded over the forest of Tunguska in Russia's northern Siberia. The object was probably either a comet nucleus or a stony asteroid. Whatever it was, it exploded about 4 miles (6 kilometers) above the ground and flattened an area of some 850 square miles (2,200 square kilometers). It was the largest-known explosion in the history of civilization. Because very few people lived near Tunguska, only two people died as a result of the blast. Had the object exploded over a crowded city, hundreds of thousands of people would have been killed and the city destroyed.

WHERE DO COMETS COME FROM?

In the Solar System, comets are the outsiders. As many as 100 billion of them seem to form a huge shell around the Sun and the planets. This shell is called the *Oort Cloud*, after the Dutch astronomer Jan H. Oort. Its inner edge lies more than 4 trillion miles (6 trillion kilometers) from the Sun. That's 45,000 times farther away than Earth is from the Sun.

Dutch astronomer Jan H. Oort's head was in the clouds. He imagined a huge shell of comets wrapped around the Solar System. Today it's called the Oort Cloud.

From time to time, the gravity of a passing star tugs a comet out of the Oort Cloud and flings it toward the Sun. The comet then takes millions of years to complete one orbit around the Sun and back out to its starting point. These comets from the Oort Cloud are called *long-period* comets.

The Oort Cloud is thought to contain billions of giant iceballs. Some are pulled out of the cloud for a long trip around the Sun (right).

31

Comet Hale-Bopp put on a wonderful show when it swept close to the Sun in 1997. Some of us will be lucky enough to see the return of Halley's Comet. Hale-Bopp, on the other hand won't be back for 2,380 years!

If a comet comes close enough to one of the gas-giant planets, such as Jupiter, it may be captured by the planet's powerful gravity. It then becomes a *short-period* comet and a member of Jupiter's *comet family*. The comet never returns to the Oort Cloud but orbits the Sun at one end and Jupiter at the other. Halley's Comet is a short-period comet that has made thirty known trips around the Sun. It was first reported as the "broom star" by Chinese astronomers in 240 B.C. Halley's most recent visit was in 1985, and the slowpoke isn't scheduled to return until 2061.

The comet with the shortest-known period is Encke. Its trip takes only three years and four months. Most short-period comets come from a huge doughnut-shaped storage area called the *Kuiper Belt*, named after the American astronomer Gerard Kuiper. About 200 million of these comets orbit the Sun in a great circular swarm near Neptune's orbit, some two hundred times Earth's distance from the Sun. Although we cannot see comets in the Oort Cloud, we can see them in the Kuiper Belt. So far, we know the orbits of more than two dozen of them.

The path of a comet. It enters the Solar System headfirst (right) and then leaves tailfirst (left). Notice how the tail is always pointing away from the Sun.

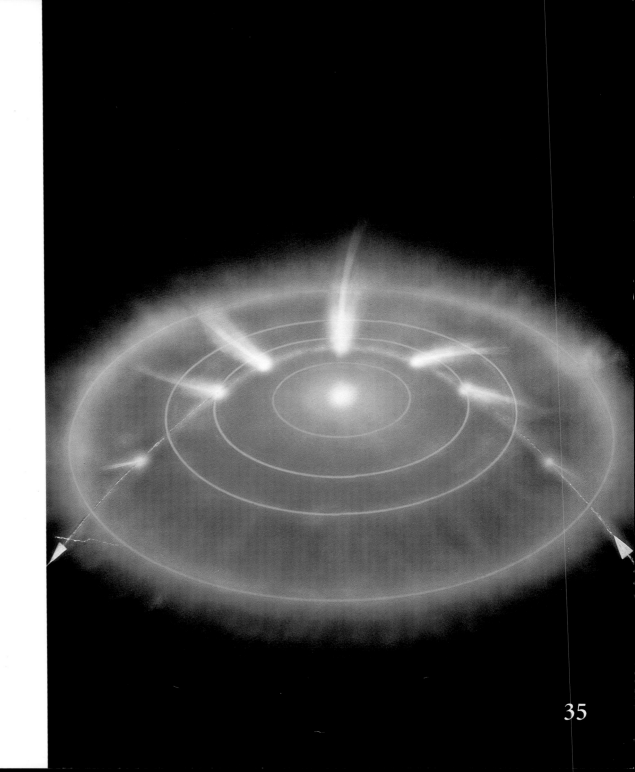

These comets whose orbits are known are about 125 miles (200 kilometers) wide. Once in a while, the tug of Neptune's gravity or one of the other giant planets hurls a Kuiper Belt comet in toward the Sun. Astronomers now think that Pluto and its moon, Charon, are actually icebergs that have been snatched out of the Kuiper Belt.

A planet that was once a comet? Pluto (top) and its moon, Charon, are something of a mystery to astronomers.

Each time a comet circles the Sun, pieces the size of sand grains flake off and stay in orbit as a cloud of comet matter. Whenever Earth passes through one of these clouds, we have a meteor shower. When a comet loses its icy matter, all that is left is a lump of rock dust.

Like a missile speeding toward its target, comet Hale-Bopp appears about to strike Tucson, Arizona. Luckily the comet was millions of miles away.

40

We now think that some of the objects we report as asteroids are really the cores of dead comets. In 1994, a train of twenty-one broken comet pieces crashed into Jupiter and put on one of the greatest displays of fireworks ever seen in the Solar System.

Cosmic fireworks. Twenty-one pieces of a dead comet crashed into Jupiter in July 1994. The Earth would not have survived their impact.

Could such an event ever happen on Earth? Comets and asteroids have crashed into our planet many times in the past, often with deadly results. Will it ever happen again? The question is not whether it will happen, but when. The next such collision may not take place for thousands of years. In the meantime, keep your eyes on the sky.

Sixty-five million years ago a giant asteroid smashed into the Gulf of Mexico. The explosion is thought to have killed off the dinosaurs and many other species.

GLOSSARY

Asteroid   Any of thousands of chunks of rock and metal fragments from the size of giant boulders to that of a train car orbiting mainly between the planets Mars and Jupiter.

Coma   The cloud of gases surrounding the nucleus of a comet.

Comet   An object mostly of ice that loops around the Sun one or more times and develops a coma gas cloud and a tail of gas and dust millions of miles long.

Comet family   Comets that have been captured by one of the gas-giant planets, such as Jupiter or Saturn, and that orbit that planet and the Sun.

Ion   An atom that has lost an electron, for example, and that is left with an electric charge. Ions may have a positive or negative electric charge.

Kuiper Belt   A region of space beyond Neptune in which a belt of comets is stored.

Long-period   Comets from the Oort Cloud that take thousands of years between repeated visits to the Sun.

Meteor   The brief streak of light seen when a piece of rock or metal from space enters Earth's atmosphere and burns up.

Meteorite   A fragment of rock or metal that enters Earth's atmosphere and strikes the ground.

Meteoroid   A fragment of rock or metal chipped off an asteroid and that stays in orbit.

Nucleus   The central core of ice that is the major part of a comet.

Oort Cloud   A storehouse of perhaps 100 billion comets forming a shell around the Sun and planets and lying some 4 trillion miles from the Sun.

Short-period   Comets that belong to comet families or that are part of the Kuiper Belt and that orbit the Sun in short amounts of time.

FIND OUT MORE

Books

Aronson, Billy. *Meteors*. Danbury, CT: Watts, 1996.

Asimov, Issac. *How Did We Find Out about Comets?* New York: Walker, 1975.

Bendick, Jeanne. *Comets and Meteors: Visitors from Space*. Brookfield, CT: Millbrook, 1991.

Carlisle, Madelyn. *Let's Investigate Magical, Mysterious Meteorites*. Hauppauge, NY: Barron, 1992.

Davis, Amanda. *Comets and Asteroids*. New York: Rosen, 1997.

Gallant, Roy A. *The Day the Sky Split Apart: The Cosmic Mystery of the Century*. New York: Simon and Schuster, 1995.

Mason, Anne. *The Dancing Meteorite*. New York: HarperCollins, 1984.

Schatz, Dennis and Yasu Osawa. *The Return of the Comet*. Seattle: Pacific Science Center, 1985.

Simon, Seymour. *Comets, Meteors, & Asteroids*. New York: Morrow, 1994.

Sipiera, Paul P. *Comets & Meteor Showers*. Danbury, CT: Childrens Press, 1997.

Sorenson, Lynda. *Comets & Meteors*. Vero Beach, FL: Rourke, 1993.

Vogt, Gregory L. *Asteroids, Comets, & Meteors*. Brookfield, CT: Millbrook, 1996.

Websites

COMETS

Let's Cook Up a Comet!
whyfiles.news.wisc.edu/011comets/crecipe.html

The Comet's Tale
cse.ssl.berkeley.edu/comod/com.html

Comets and Meteors: The Differences
medicine.wustl.edu/~kronkg/differ.html

ASTEROIDS

The Impact Catastrophe Electronic Picturebook
www.stsci.edu/exined/Impact.html

Asteroid Photo Gallery
nssd.gsfc.nasa.gov/photo_gallery/photogallery-asteroids.html

The Asteroid Belt
www.tcsn.net/afiner/asteroid.htm

METEORS

Meteors and Their Properties
meteorites.lpl.arizona.edu

Meteoroids and Meteorites
www.hawastsoc.org/solar/eng/meteor.htm

Meteors—Interactive Animation
liftoff.msfc.nasa.gov/academy/space/solarsystem/meteors/meteors.html

AUTHOR'S BIO

Roy A. Gallant, called "one of the deans of American science writers for children" by *School Library Journal*, is the author of more than eighty books on scientific subjects. Since 1979, he has been director of the Southworth Planetarium at the University of Southern Maine, where he holds an adjunct full professorship. He lives in Rangeley, Maine.

INDEX

Page numbers for illustrations are in boldface.